A Healthy Life Work Book

BY CHELSEA KONG

© 2021 Chelsea Kong

All rights reserved. All images used in this book are licensed copies from their respectful owners including Freepik and Unsplash. This book or any portion thereof may not be reproduced or used in any manner whatsoever without the express written permission of the publisher except for the use of brief quotations in a book review.

Printed in 2021, Made in Toronto, Canada
ISBN: 978-1-990399-13-8
Library and Archives Canada

Please make sure to get a copy of
A Healthy Life book to use this workbook.

Just to say thanks, you can get a free book here:
https://chelseak532002550.wordpress.com/books-for-sharing/

"'But then I will bring health and heal the people there. I will let them enjoy peace and safety.
(Jeremiah 33:6 ICB)

Live right, eat right, and drink right.

Use what you learn to change your life.

It's easy to do and teach others.

MAKE A PLAN

Most people eat three times a day.

Think about all the food and drink for each meal.

Breakfast, lunch, and dinner.

Some people have small snacks too.

BREAKFAST

What food would you eat for breakfast?

Write on paper a healthy meal you can eat.

You can have different food each day.

What about a drink to go with it?

SAMPLE BREAKFAST

How about lightly fried eggs made in butter?

Avocado, eggs with cheese inside, and tomato.

A glass of milk or freshly-made juice.

Sounds healthy. Do you agree?

LUNCH

What kind of food would be good for lunch?

Write down on paper what you want to eat.

It can be heavy like a hotpot,
many dishes, or light like a salad.

What about a drink to go with it like
water, juice, or a smoothie?

SAMPLE LUNCH

How about fresh fruits and salad with nuts?

How about a baked potato with butter?

Your salad can have chickpea, salt, pepper, and lemon for sauce.

Avocado, plain Greek yogurt, cilantro, olive oil, lime juice, garlic, salt, and pepper is another way.

DINNER

Most people eat more for dinner, but to be healthy it's better to eat less or eat early.

What about a drink to go with it?

Most people eat more for dinner, but to be healthy it's better to eat less or eat early.

What about a drink to go with it?

SAMPLE DINNER

How about chicken, vegetables, and rice?

How about beef, carrots, broccoli, and rice?

Water or a tea that you make from fruits, nuts, flowers, or vegetables.

Milk or soup is okay too.

SNACKS

Nuts

Yogurt

Seeds

Vegetables and Healthy Dips

Fruits

SMOOTHIE DRINK

Yogurt and Milk

Banana

Blueberry

Strawberry

A little bit of Honey and Cinnamon

FRESH AND RAW

Fresh food is better for you.

Eat raw food more than cooked food.

It keeps the vitamins and minerals inside.

It makes the body strong.

SOME EXAMPLES

Sushi

Salad

Sandwiches

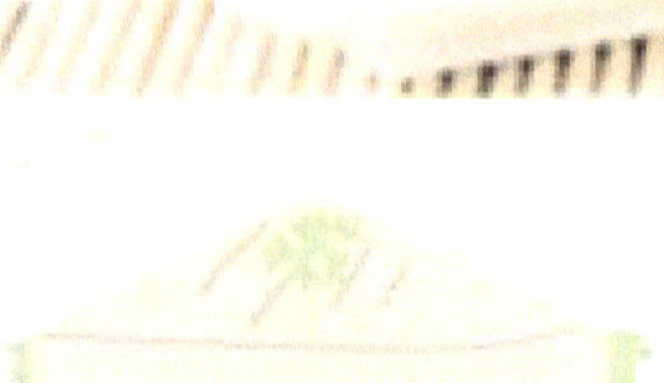

BEST WAYS TO COOK

Steam

Slow-cooked

Boiled

WAYS TO COOK

Baked

Grilled

Roasted

Lightly toasted or oven cooked

STAY AWAY FROM

Fried

Overcooked/Burned

Microwaved

Margarin

Coke, Pepsi, pop, soda, and junk food.

Candies and sweet desserts with lots of sugar.

Canned and MSG

HOW TO DRINK

How would you make a healthy drink?

Think of the different drinks in
A Healthy Life book.

What healthy drink do daddy and
mommy have in the morning?

Write it down below:

_____

COFFEE

These will help adults to have the energy to do their job.

Did you know there are different kinds of coffee?

Arabica

Decaf

Regular

SPECIAL COFFEE

Latte (made with Expresso and steamed milk)

Mocha (Coffee with hot chocolate, milk, and whipped cream)

Expresso

Iced Cappuccino
(coffee made sweet, crushed ice, and cream).

Ice Coffee
(coffee made sweet, cream, and ice).

WHAT CAN YOU DO?

Special coffee drinks may have lots of sugar sweet.

There are different kinds of sugar too.

You can use Agave syrup.

WHAT CAN YOU DO?

What can you use that is better than sugar?

1. _____

2. _____

3. _____

4. _____

PREPARING MEAT

How does your daddy or mommy prepare meat?

_____

_____

_____

_____

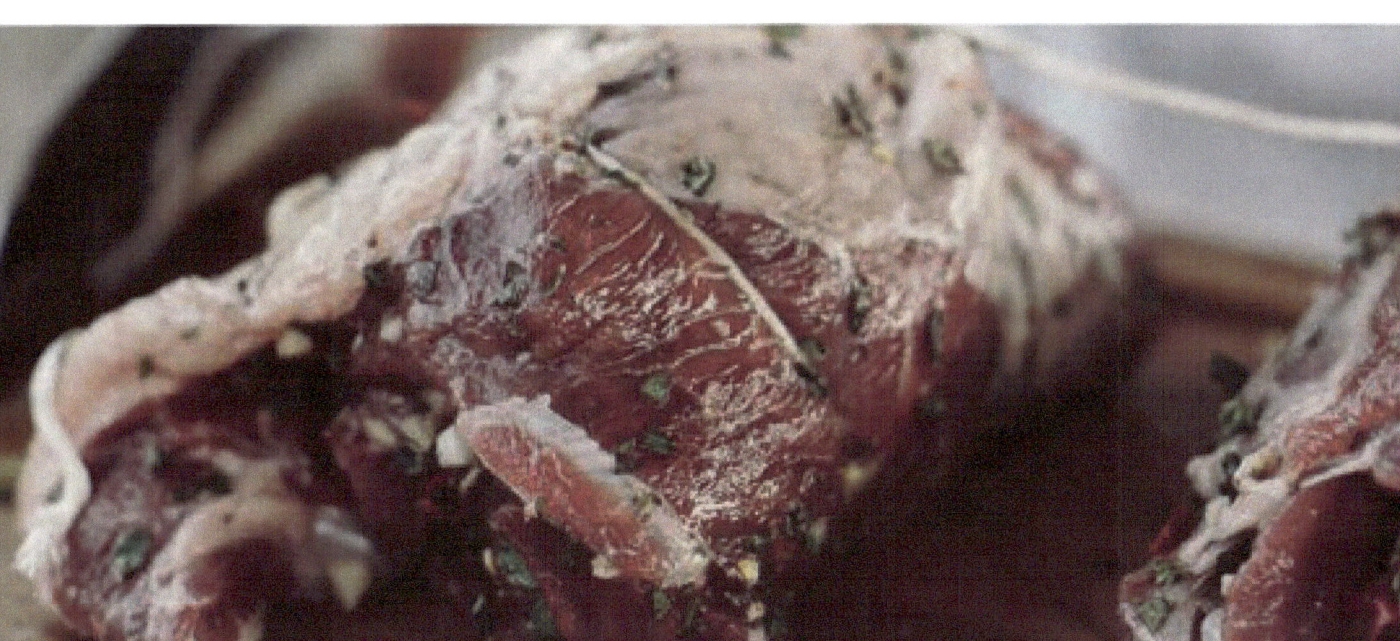

There are many ways to do it.

Each family does it differently.

PREPARING BEEF (CHINESE)

Sesame oil

Salt

Pepper

Garlic

Soya sauce

Cornstarch

A little bit of baking soda to make it soft.

EGGS

What other ways can you make eggs?

Try to think of better ways to eat them.

Dr. Joel Wallach said we should have at least 2 eggs every day.

How many do you eat?

USE THIS PAGE TO WRITE

BEST WAYS TO EAT EGGS

Poach (not more than 212 degrees).

Scrambled with butter over low heat.

Soft Boil (2 minutes).

Raw

EGG NOG RECIPE

Eggs

Honey (a little bit)

Milk

Cream

Cinnamon

Vinegar extract

Nutmeg

RED WINE

Adults also drink red wine.

It goes well with red meat and is healthy.

It is made of grapes made into wine.

There are other drinks for adults, but they should not drink too much.

NAME OF JUICES

1. _____

2. _____

3. _____

NAME OF WATER

Do you remember the names of the water that are good for you?

1. _____

2. _____

3. _____

SOME TEAS

Dandelion leaf and root

Mint

Can you name two others?

1. _____

2. _____

LARD

Do you remember the names of the water that are good for you?

1. _____

2. _____

3. _____

It is healthy to use lard.

What can you cook with lard?

_____

_____

SOME OF THE BEST SPICES

Tumeric

Rosemary

Basil

Nutmeg

Saffron

Cinnamon

TYPES OF VITAMINS AND MINERALS

Do you remember the different kinds of vitamins and minerals you can eat? There are three.

Which ones are the best to take?

1. _____

2. _____

HOW MANY VITAMINS?

How many vitamins are there? They start with letters of the alphabet.

_ _ _ _ _

Name some fruit that you eat.

1. _ _ _ _ _ _ _ _ _ _ _ _ _ _ _ _ _

2. _ _ _ _ _ _ _ _ _ _ _ _ _ _ _ _ _

3. _ _ _ _ _ _ _ _ _ _ _ _ _ _ _ _ _

4. _ _ _ _ _ _ _ _ _ _ _ _ _ _ _ _ _

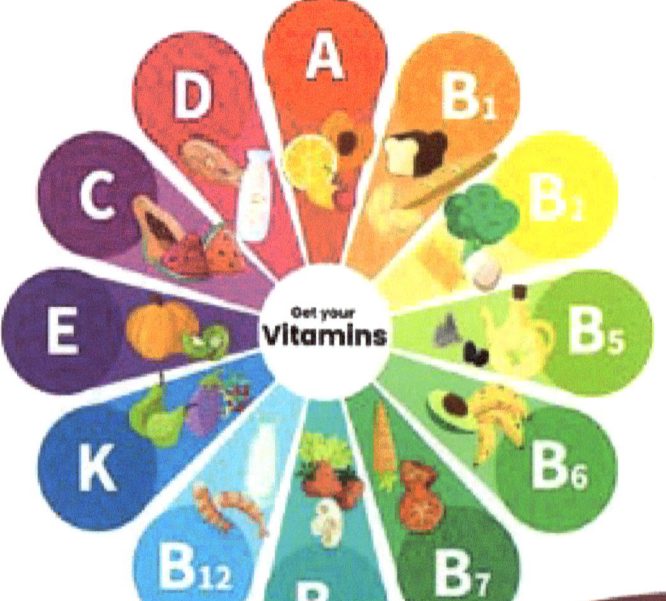

MINERALS AND MORE

How many essential minerals and more that we need?

Who is the doctor that talks about this?

SUNLIGHT

How long do you need to be in the sun?

What vitamin does the sun give us?

EXERCISE

Write them out and do one each day:

SLEEP

How many hours of sleep should you have?

Try to sleep early at night.
Do you wake up early too?

ACTIVITY TIME

Let's try to see what happens. Ask your daddy and mommy first to do this with you.

Take two steaks, a bowl of Coca-Cola, a healthy marinade, or oil.

One steak inside of a bowl of Coca Cola and the other steak inside of a healthy marinade or oil. The steak will be used as the body.

Leave them in there for 3 days and see what happens.

You should see one steak begin to go bad. That shows what happens when we put unhealthy foods in our bodies.

What about the steak that is in the healthy oil or marinade?

This shows what happens when we eat healthily.

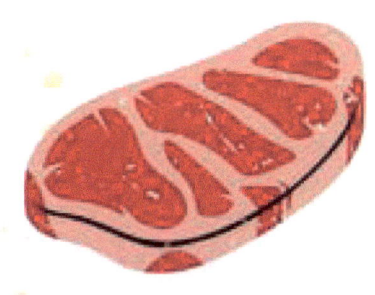

TAKE THE CHALLENGE: DAY 1

Let's track each day the healthy meals and drinks.

Start eating one healthy meal and drink today.

Write it on a blank page.

You should know that your body is a temple for the Holy Spirit. The Holy Spirit is in you. You have received the Holy Spirit from God. You do not own yourselves. 20 You were bought by God for a price. So honor God with your bodies. (1 Cor. 6:19-20)

CHALLENGE DAY 1: WRITE IT HERE

Meal of the Day:

_____

_____

_____

_____

_____

_____

_____

_____

TAKE THE CHALLENGE: DAY 2

Choose a healthy snack to eat today.

Choose a new healthy drink than yesterday.

The new healthy meal today.

So if you eat, or if you drink, or if you do anything, do everything for the glory of God. (1 Corinthians 10:31 ICB)

CHALLENGE DAY 2: WRITE IT HERE

Healthy Meal, Snack, and Drink:

TAKE THE CHALLENGE: DAY 3

Choose an exercise to start to do today.

Eat a new healthy snack.

Keep eating a healthy meal each day.

Read your Bible and pray more.

Training your body helps you in some ways, but serving God helps you in every way. Serving God brings you blessings in this life and in the future life, too. (1 Timothy 4:8 ICB)

CHALLENGE DAY 3: WRITE IT HERE

Healthy Meal, Snack, and Drink:

_____

_____

_____

_____

_____

_____

_____

_____

CHALLENGE DAY 3: WRITE IT HERE

Exercise:

Bible and Prayer:

TAKE THE CHALLENGE: DAY 4

Drink a cup of water and stop eating junk food.

Go outside in the sun to play for at least 15 minutes.

Take time to laugh more.

CHALLENGE DAY 4:

Eat two healthy meals each day.

A happy heart is like good medicine.
But a broken spirit drains your strength. (Proverbs 17:22)

CHALLENGE DAY 4: WRITE IT HERE

How long did you go outside?

Did you take time to laugh?

Did you drink water and stop eating junk food?

CHALLENGE DAY 4: WRITE IT HERE

Exercise:

Bible and Prayer:

CHALLENGE DAY 4: WRITE IT HERE

Healthy Meal, Snack, and Drink:

TAKE THE CHALLENGE: DAY 5

Drink a new healthy drink.

Try to eat raw vegetables with one meal.

Eat plain yogurt and add your own fruit.

Obey God's Word like what your daddy and mommy tell you to do.

I will bring back your health. And I will heal your injuries," says the Lord. (Jeremiah 30:17a ICB)

CHALLENGE DAY 5: OBEYING GOD'S WORD

what did you obey from God's Word?

CHALLENGE DAY 5: WRITE IT HERE

Healthy Meal, Snack, and Drink:

_____

_____

_____

_____

_____

_____

_____

_____

CHALLENGE DAY 5: WRITE IT HERE

Exercise:

_____

_____

Bible and Prayer:

_____

_____

_____

_____

TAKE THE CHALLENGE: DAY 6

Make sure you sleep 6-8 hours a day.

Eat non-meat food for one meal.

Have one more fruit.

Remember one scripture and do it each day.

The Lord will take away all disease from you. You will not have the terrible diseases that were in Egypt. But he will give them to your enemies.
(Deuteronomy 7:15 ICB)

CHALLENGE DAY 6: WRITE IT HERE

Healthy Meal, Snack, and Drink:

TAKE THE CHALLENGE: DAY 7

Eat three healthy meals and drinks today.

Drink another cup of water.

Have another new healthy snack.

TAKE THE CHALLENGE: DAY 7

My child, pay attention to my words. Listen closely to what I say. Don't ever forget my words. Keep them deep within your heart. These words are the secret to life for those who find them. They bring health to the whole body. (Proverbs 4:20-22 ICB)

Please send me your 7 days of challenge and share it on my Facebook found near the end of the book.

TAKE THE CHALLENGE: DAY 7

Be very careful about what you think. Your thoughts run through your life. Don't use your mouth to tell lies. Don't ever say things that are not true. Keep your eyes focused on what is right. Keep looking straight ahead to what is good. Be careful what you do. Always do what is right. Do not do anything unless it is right. Stay away from evil. (Proverbs 4:23-27)

CHALLENGE DAY 7: WRITE IT HERE

How many cups of water did you drink?

_ _ _ _ _ _ _ _

New Healthy snack:

_ _

_ _

_ _

CHALLENGE DAY 7: WRITE IT HERE

Healthy Meal, Snack, and Drink:

_____

_____

_____

_____

_____

_____

_____

_____

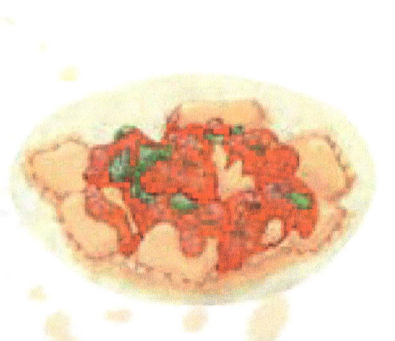

CHALLENGE DAY 7: WRITE IT HERE

Exercise:

_ _

_ _

Bible and Prayer:

_ _

_ _

_ _

_ _

Certificate
for Achievement

Proudly Presented to:

----

for completing A Healthy Life 7 Days Challenge!

Chelsea Kong

SALVATION PRAYER

God, I know I sinned against you. Forgive me for the wrong that I have done. I believe that Jesus Christ died on the cross for me. That He rose from the grave after three days so that I can have His long-lasting life. Come into my heart to be my Lord and Savior. I choose to turn away from my sins and I choose to follow you. Lead me to walk with you. Keep me safe and teach me your ways. Stop every bad thing in my life that has an open door to hurt me. Close those doors. Holy Spirit fill me now in Jesus' name. Amen.

BAPTISM IN THE HOLY SPIRIT

Jesus, you are the one that fills me with Your Spirit. Come Holy Spirit and come into my life and fill me to overflow with Your presence. Come with your fire too. Thank you for the gift of tongues in Jesus' name. Amen.

BAPTISM IN THE HOLY SPIRIT

Open your mouth and let the words come out that God gives you. It will be words that you don't know what they mean. You can ask God what it means. You need to let Him talk through you every day to grow this gift. He will bring you closer to God and you will know Jesus more. You will have power from God to do great things and know things.

PRAYER

Father, help me to use what I learn from this book to live healthy every day. Teach me how to eat, drink, and what to do each day. Show me how to be like Jesus in all that I do. Teach me from your word how to live a clean and healthy life with you in Jesus' name. Amen.

MESSAGE FROM THE AUTHOR

Be blessed with divine health and prosperity in every area of your life. Please use the 7 days challenge every day. It takes 21 days for it to do it well. Then you will always be healthy. You can find out more about healthy foods to eat from Dr. Joel Wallach and there may be others who know about the food that people sometimes call superfood too. Our bones need collagen to make them strong and healthy, which you can get from Knox Gelatin. You can also have beef gelatin too. It's great for soup.

A Healthy Life Facebook Group:
https://www.facebook.com/groups/ahealthylifegroup/

OTHER PRODUCTS

Knowing God
How to Hear God's Voice
New Life in Jesus
Loving Israel
God's Gifts
Meeting God
Word Power
Fruit of the Spirit
The Tabernacle
Bride for Jesus
A Life of Prayer
Live Free
Who am I in Jesus
Walk in Love
God's Favor
Man of God
Woman of God
How to Use Money
God's Wisdom
Fasting
See Jerusalem and Bethany
First Fruit Offering
Feast of Trumpets
Day of Atonement
Feast of Tabernacles
Counting the Omer
Festival of Lights
Glory, Presence, and Holy Spirit
Live in God's Presence

Pentecost
31 Day Devotional
Biblical Puzzle Book Vol 1
Biblical Puzzle Book Vol 2
Biblical Puzzle Book Vol 3
Biblical Puzzle Book Vol 4
Biblical Puzzle Book Vol 5
Bible Puzzles for Young Children Book 1
Bible Puzzles for Young Children Book 2
Bible Puzzles for Young Children Book 3
Biblical Puzzles for Children Book 1-3
How God Speaks
Knowing Jesus
Knowing Holy Spirit
Hear God Speak

Teaching Series
How to Hear God's Voice Teaching Guide & Audio Book
Relationship with God, Jesus, Holy Spirit Guide
Knowing God, Jesus, Holy Spirit Guide & Audio Book

More coming soon!

More books on Amazon, Kobo, and Barnes and Noble
https://www.amazon.com/author/chelseakong

Please leave a review to help the author continue to write more books to reach more readers. Thank you so much for your support.

About
CHELSEA KONG

She is a writer, creative arts and digital media artist, skilled administration professional, and podcaster. Chelsea also served in a variety of roles, from audiovisual, photography, to assisting on the worship team, and ministry team. She also has a passion for families being united.

Chelsea graduated from Hotel and Restaurant Management, Digital Media Arts, Office Administration, and experience working with children. She mainly writes children's books, stories, bridal writing, poems, lyrics for songs, words of encouragement, blessings, prayers, and jokes. The author of How to Hear the Voice of God, the Bridal Collection, Knowing God, etc. She also has her own Bible Puzzle books and other inspired products. Her podcast channel is called Chelsea K on Anchor, Spotify, and iTunes. She has been on Unity Live Radio and The Lady Tracey Show and is highly recommended by a Proud Christian blog.

Please check my website to find out more:
https://chelseak532002550.wordpress.com/

REFERENCES

Wallach, Joel, Dr. "The 90 Essential Nutrients." The Wallach Revolution, 2015, https://thewallachrevolution.com/

Biblegateway, NIV, ICB. N/A, https://www.biblegateway.com/

Healthline. "8 Simple and Healthy Salad Dressings: Avocado lime." Healthline, 2005-2021. https://www.healthline.com/nutrition/healthy-salad-dressing#TOC_TITLE_HDR_4

Wallach, Joel, Dr. "Dr. Wallach - 10 Bad Foods to Avoid No Junk Food." Youngevity, https://youngofficial.com/dr-wallach-10-bad-foods-to-avoid/

www.ingramcontent.com/pod-product-compliance
Lightning Source LLC
Chambersburg PA
CBHW042056050526
44107CB00110B/1192